SMIRK
Over 1450 Smiles for Your Face

Agnes Franz, Editor

authorHOUSE™

1663 LIBERTY DRIVE, SUITE 200
BLOOMINGTON, INDIANA 47403
(800) 839-8640
WWW.AUTHORHOUSE.COM

First published by AuthorHouse 12/19/05

ISBN: 1-4208-8444-1 (sc)

Printed in the United States of America
Bloomington, Indiana

This book is printed on acid-free paper.

INTRODUCTION

Here's a book with a sense of humor. *Smirk* is a casual compilation of quotes, clichés and off-the-top-of-the-head wit, wisdom and fun to put a smile on your face. Let it amuse and inspire. You know how some clever ideas begin with "They say…" There's that kind of humor here, as well. The editor works to move you from the day's doldrums to a lighter level, escaping accountability.

There's no formal organization. Some quotes are attributed to their producers; many come from the comics, classic literature, editorials, or bumper stickers. Some remain anonymous because the person who first said them wasn't willing to own up to issuing the words.

Any morsel you find in this book might be snarky, smiley, sanctimonious, sentimental, sacred, irreverent, tender, cheeky, classic or even reasonable. Material has been researched in library stacks, in barrooms, in college classrooms, on the internet as well as at kitchen tables.

Brief quotes and adages and a few very short poems are selected for a quick read. Here and there you find material that goes back to *once upon a time*. This is a mixture of topics, visions and viewpoints. We can hardly call it an anthology— it is not at all scholarly.

The objective is pure escapism.

<>

THE BEST THINGS IN LIFE ARE FREE BUT NO LONGER AVAILABLE.

If the worm turns—go fishing.

Artificial intelligence is no match for natural stupidity.

Any idiot can face a crisis—it's this day-to-day living that wears you out.

—Anton Chekhov

Being happy is too important to be left to chance.

—Robert Rodale

The first human being who hurled an insult instead of a stone was the founder of civilization.

—Sigmund Freud

You can't empty a wastebasket once and for all.

Creativity is allowing yourself to make mistakes. Art is knowing which to keep.

—Scott Adams

Nothing a magician does can't be done by a 10-year-old—with 15 years of practice.

The problem with the gene pool is that there is no lifeguard.

EARTH LAUGHS IN FLOWERS.
–RALPH WALDO EMERSON

Hospitality— The virtue which induces us to feed and lodge certain persons who are not in need of food and lodging.

The average person thinks he isn't.   —Father Lorenzoni

SMIRK

To see a world in a grain of sand,
And a heaven in wild flower,
Hold infinity in the palm of your had,
And eternity in an hour.

—William Blake

If work is so terrific, how come they have to pay us to
do it?

Silences make the real conversations between friends. Not
the saying but the never needing to say is what counts.

—Margaret Lee Runbeck

The house is the picture of the soul, the garment
of the will.

We need to put up with two or three caterpillars
if we want to get to know the butterflies.

Take time for yourself.

Mistrust makes life difficult. Trust makes it risky.

IF YOU'RE GOING THROUGH HELL, KEEP GOING.

```
Every wakeful step, every mindful
act is the direct path to awakening.
Wherever you go, there you are.
                              —Buddha
```

Follow your bliss.

Dance as though no one is watching you. Love as though you have never been hurt before. Sing as though no one can hear you. Live as though heaven is on earth.

If you want a taxi in New York City, buy one !

Idiot—a member of a large and powerful tribe whose influence in human affairs has always been dominant and controlling.

What a wonderful world! —Louis Armstrong

To get a dog to do what you want, you give it a command.
To get a cat to do what you want, you give it a suggestion.

I don't need a memory. I have an imagination.

If cats could talk, they would lie to you.   —Rob Kopack

I'M TRYING TO BECOME THE PERSON MY DOG THINKS I AM.

Rational—devoid of all delusions save those of observation, experience and reflection.

The past is a foreign country; they do things differently there.

Love makes men just, simple, pure, rich, wise and contented, and with its sweetness lessens every grief.

If you are not the lead dog the view never changes.

Gossip is when you hear something you like about someone you don't.

—Earl Wilson

A friend is someone who understands your past, believes in your future, and accepts you today just the way you are.

Try not to hurt a pal; this might be the only one of that kind we have.

Please do not breathe while I smoke.

Life is a moderately good play with a badly written third
act.

—Truman Capote

WOE TO HIM THAT READS BUT ONE BOOK.

With money in your pocket, you are wise
and you are handsome and you sing well,
too,

The nail that sticks up gets hammered down.

—Japanese proverb

A woman is a sovereign, having eminence and
supremacy over loyal subjects who adore her or else.

Never economize on luxuries.

Striving for excellence motivates you; striving for perfection
is demoralizing.

To get peace, if you want, make yourself a nest of pleasant thoughts to curl up inside each night.

—John Ruskin

May your neighbors respect you, trouble neglect you, and the angels protect you and heaven accept you.

...and thou shalt have dominion over the animals—except the cats.

No man is lonely while eating spaghetti. It requires too much attention.

—Christopher Morley

DO ONE THING EVERY DAY THAT SCARES YOU.

The first rule is to keep an untroubled spirit. The second is to look things in the face and know them for what they are.

—Marcus Aurelius

Everyone is born right-handed. Only the gifted overcome it.

Do Justice, love kindness and walk humbly with your dog.

Because NICE matters, that's why.

Nothing is worth more than this day. — Goethe

Our success is measured by willingness to keep trying.

It seems that if there were any logic to our language, trust would be a four-letter word.

Age doesn't matter unless you're a cheese.

The ornament of a house is the friends who frequent it.

FLOWERS ARE THE HIEROGLYPHICS OF ANGELS.

The whole world is full of things, and somebody has to look for them.

Why do people with closed minds always open their mouths?

Kind words can be short and easy to speak, but their echoes are truly endless.

—Mother Teresa

A balanced diet is a cookie in each hand.

There comes a time in life when we get to wonder which is the lesser of two evils—age or weight.

As a traveler who has once been from home is wiser than he who has never left his own doorstop.

— Margaret Mead

He lives doubly who also enjoys the past.

——Marcus Martial

We're born crying, why not die laughing.

Sometimes the key to happiness is not assuming it's locked in the first place.

MY MIND IS LIKE A STEEL WHATCHAMACALLIT.

Ode to a Kid Grown Up
I'm sorry you are wiser,
I'm sorry you are taller,
I liked you better foolish
And I liked you better smaller.

Stressed spelled backwards is DESSERTS !

An optimist is a person who sees a green light everywhere, while the pessimist sees only the red stoplight. A truly wise person is color-blind.

— Albert Schweitzer

If you were born without wings, do nothing to prevent them growing.

—Coco Chanel

Flowers leave some of their fragrance in the hand that bestows them.

Do what you feel in your heart to be right—for you'll be criticized anyway.

Good friends are like angels—you don't have to see them to know they are there.

Gardeners spread the best dirt.

If you're lucky enough to be in the mountains, you're lucky enough.

BEER IS PROOF THAT GOD LOVES US AND WANTS US TO BE HAPPY.

       —BEN FRANKLIN

When I get tired of shopping I sit down and try on shoes.

I'd give up chocolate, but I'm no quitter.

Yesterday is history, tomorrow is a mystery, today is a gift and that's why we call it the Present.

The ultimate inspiration is the deadline.

The reason grandparents and grandchildren get along so well is that they have a common enemy.

       —Sam Levenson

Grant me the senility to forget the people I never liked, the good fortune to run into the people I do like, the eyesight to tell the difference.

Unfortunately, many people do not consider fun an important item on their daily agenda.
— Gen Chuck Yeager

If you are kind, people may accuse you of ulterior motives. Be kind, anyway.

A happy life is just a string of happy moments. But most people don't allow the happy moment because they are so busy trying to get a happy life.

LAUGHTER IS BRIGHTEST IN THE PLACE WHERE FOOD IS.
—IRISH PROVERB

When a man criticizes his wife's taste
he may overlook the fact that she chose
him as her husband.

Because I'm the Mother; that's why !

The world is a stage, but the play is badly cast.

—Oscar Wilde

I thought I worked my butt off, but it followed me home.

I have no time to grow old...I'm too busy for that.

— Geo. MacDonald

There are those who take paths, and those who make them.

Leave no stone unturned. You might be surprised how many opportunities crawl out.

Where did we go wrong?

People who do not get into scrapes are a great deal less interesting than those who do.
—Murasaki Shikibu

LIFE IS TOO SHORT TO DRINK BAD WINE.

Indulge your imagination in every possible flight.
—Jane Austen

Curiosity is one of the permanent and certain characteristics of a vigorous mind.
— Samuel Johnson

When you are old, nothing is bad or outrageous. Either you have done it or wish you had.

Some ideas are so stupid, only intellectuals believe them.

—H.G. Wells

The art of being wise is the art of knowing what to overlook.

Hope is a thing with feathers. —Emily Dickinson

Go confidently in the direction of your dreams.

—Thoreau

If the shoe fits...buy it in every color.

We make a living by what we get; we make a life by what we give.

GRATITUDE CAN TURN A MEAL INTO A FEAST, A HOUSE INTO A HOME, A STRANGER INTO A FRIEND.

Hold fast your dreams! Within your
heart keep one still, secret spot where
dreams may go and may thrive and grow
where doubt and fear are not. Keep
a place apart within your heart, for
little dreams to go.

— Louise Driscoll.

Charm is a way of getting the answer Yes without having asked any clear question.

— Albert Camus

There are two kinds of babies in the world: the cute, cuddly, cherubic bundles of joy and the real ones.

Time is a great healer but a lousy beautician.

Admiration is our polite recognition of another's resemblance to ourselves.

—Ambrose Bierce

I don't want to achieve immortality through my work. I want to achieve it through not dying.
                                        —Woody Allen

Age doesn't always bring wisdom—sometimes it comes alone.

We turn not older with years, but newer every day.

                                        —Emily Dickinson

The kiss of the sun for pardon, the song of the birds for mirth, you are nearer God's heart in a garden than anywhere else on earth.

WOE TO HIM THAT READS BUT ONE BOOK.

By simply being ourselves, we don't have to move mountains or make miracles...but sometimes we do anyway.

Sometimes the heart sees what is invisible to the eyes.

Man is troubled by what might be called the "Dog Wish" a strange and involved compulsion to be as happy and carefree as a dog.

—James Thurber

Your life is the answer to someone's prayers.

Time is too slow for those who wait, too swift for those who fear, too long for those who grieve, too short for those who rejoice, but for those who love—time is eternity.

—Henry VanDyke

Blessings come in many ways and the nicest come as friends.

Beauty, truth, friendship, love, creation—these
are the great values of life. We can't prove them,
or explain them, yet they are the most stable
things in our lives.

—Jesse Holmes

Every Wall is a Door.

NEVER TRUST ANYONE WHO DOESN'T LIKE DOGS.

In the hope of reaching the moon men
fail to see the flowers that blossom at
their feet.

—Albert Schweitzer

Practice the art of doing nothing.

Masquerading as a normal person day after day is
exhausting.

It's not the years in your life that count. It's the life in your years.

Live well, love much, laugh often.

If we take care of the moments, the years will take care of themselves.

Life is sacred: live on purpose, be intoxicated with this world and astonished with the world you imagine.

Growth is a journey...success doesn't require arrival.

Inside every older woman is a younger woman—
wondering what the hell happened.

—Cora H. Armstrong

EMBRACE MOMENTS OF GRACE. GIVE THE CHILD
IN YOU A WIDE SKIP.

Style is what kicks in when charm
fails.

The hardest years in life are those between ten and seventy.
—Helen Hayes

We do not inherit the earth from our ancestors; we
borrow it from our children.

Book lovers never go to bed alone.

Things are going to get a lot worse before they get worse.
—Lily Tomlin

When they want to overpay you there is usually
a reason.

I have yet to hear a man ask for advice on how to
combine marriage and a career.

—Gloria Steinem

Never fear being vulgar, just boring
—Diana Vreeland

Enjoy money while you have it. There are no pockets in shrouds.

STYLE IS WHAT YOU ARE INSIDE.

The ornament of a house is the friends who frequent it.

—Emerson

There's more to life than work !

Live! Live! Life is a banquet, and most poor suckers are starving to death.

—Rosalind Russell

Never fry bacon in the nude!

It's not the houses I love; it's the life I live in them.

—Coco Chanel

A gal needs uncommon modesty to resist the delight of being called the most charming girl in the world.

Why not be oneself? That is the whole secret of a successful appearance. If one is a greyhound, why try to look like a Pekinese?

—Dame Edith Sitwell

The way to avoid housework is to live in a tent.

There ain't no time for lookin' pretty when you gotta slop the pigs.

EVEN THE LONE RANGER DIDN'T GO IT ALONE.

Each day is too short for all the
thoughts I want to think, all the walks
I want to take, all the books I want to
read, and all the friends I want to see.
—John Burroughs

Only the mediocre are always at their best.

If all the world is a stage, where is the audience
sitting?

When planning, the shortest pencil is worth more than the
longest memory.

If you try to fail, and succeed, which have you
done?

First, don't sweat the small stuff. Second, it's all
small stuff.

— Dr. Robt. Eliot

Failure is the opportunity to begin again more intelligently.

—Henry Ford

If they say 'You can't take it with you,' they're probably trying to take it from you.

—Robert Orben

IF TODAY WERE A DRESS, I'D RETURN IT.

Throughout history, the most common debilitating human ailment has been cold feet!

—Cervantes

No one really knows enough to be a pessimist.

—Norman Cousins

It's not the size of the dog in a fight; it's the size of the fight in the dog.

–Kit Raymond

Don't stay in bed unless you make money in bed.

—–George Burns

You don't have to be born beautiful to be wildly attractive.

—Diana Vreeland

Dreams are like feathers. If you have enough you can fly.

He without benefit of scruples...his fun and money soon quadruples.

—Ogden Nash

We do not remember days...we remember moments.

If you want to improve—be content to be thought of as being stupid and foolish.

WHEN IN DANGER OR IN DOUBT
RUN IN CIRCLES, SCREAM AND SHOUT.

That we are not much sicker and much
madder than we are is due exclusively
to that most blessed and blessing of
all natural graces—sleep.
—Adous Huxley

Life is a great big canvas; throw all the paint on it you can.
—Danny Kaye

Who knows? The IRS may have an office at the end of
the rainbow.

I am still learning. —Michaelangelo

How old would you be if you did not know how
old you are?

I'd kill for a Nobel Peace Prize.

Half the people you know are below average.

Deep peace of the running water to you,
Deep peace of the flowing air to you,
Deep peace of the quiet earth to you,
Deep peace of the shining stars to you.
                              —*Celtic benediction*

NEVER SEPARATE THE LIFE YOU LIVE FROM THE
WORDS YOU SPEAK.

A lot of what we experience as strength
comes from knowing what to do with
weakness.
                    —Barbara Ehrenreich

Never get so busy making a living that you forget to make a
life.

A conscience is what hurts when all your other parts feel so good.

Borrow money from pessimists—they never expect it back.

You shall know the truth, and the truth shall make you mad as hell.

—Aldous Huxley

How do you know when you're out of invisible ink?

The early bird may get the worm, but the second mouse gets the cheese.

When everything is coming your way, you're probably driving in the wrong lane.

AMBITION IS A POOR EXCUSE FOR NOT HAVING
ENOUGH SENSE TO BE LAZY.

Hard work pays off in the future,
laziness pays off immediately.

If at first you don't succeed, destroy all evidence that you
tried.

A conclusion is the spot where you got tired of trying
to think something through.

Why do psychics have to ask you for your name?

The universe is like a safe to which there is a combination;
but the combination is locked in the safe.

—Peter DeVries

The hardness of the butter is proportional to
the softness of the bread.

To steal ideas from one person is plagiarism; to steal from many is research.

Experience is something you don't get until just after you need it.

The sooner you fall behind, the more time you'll have to catch up.

THERE NEVER WAS A GOOD KNIFE MADE OF BAD STEEL.

—BENJAMIN FRANKLIN

A clear conscience is usually the sign of a bad memory.

The face of a man gives us fuller and more interesting information than his tongue.

—Di Schopenhauer

The more joy we have, the more nearly perfect we are.

—de Spinoza

Life is a jigsaw puzzle with half the pieces missing.

When you live in a place you've always lived in you get to see things not only in space, but in time.

—Shirley Ann Grau

Second marriage is triumph of hope over experience.

—Samuel Johnson

One may be as brisk as a bee in conversation, but with pencil in hand becomes totally paralyzed.

In human relations kindness and lies are worth a thousand truths.

—Graham Greene

A lie can travel halfway around the world while the truth
is putting on its shoes.

—Mark Twain

MEN MADE CIVILIZATION IN ORDER TO IMPRESS
THEIR GIRLFRIENDS.

—ORSON WELLS

Life is short. Make fun of it !

These days children are getting older at a much younger
age.

It's never too late to be what you might have been.

—George Eliot

My mind works like lightning, one brilliant flash and
it's gone.

Life is a disease brought on through sex and ultimately
resulting in death.

Experience is the shortest distance between
anticipation and regret.

—Peter DeVries

You know you're getting old when you order a
three-minute egg in a restaurant and they ask for
money up front.

"Good morning" is an oxymoron.

No matter how serious your life requires you to be;
everyone needs a friend to act goofy with.

GIVE ADVICE WHEN IT IS REQUESTED OR WHEN IT
IS A LIFE THREATENING SITUATION.

Keep words both soft and tender because
tomorrow you may have to eat them.

Don't talk unless you can improve the silence.

—Ben Franklin

Fill what's empty. Empty what's full. And scratch where it itches.

If this world is all about winners, what's for losers?

Life is not always kind, but sometimes it does go out of its way to ignore a person.

We know that life is tough, but be tougher.

Do one thing each day that makes you happy.

Never relax, never give in—pull in those longings and stick out that chin.

—Neil Simon

A hard core control freak is a grammarian who won't even allow nouns and verbs to agree.

I'VE GOT A GOOD MIND TO GIVE UP LIVING AND GO SHOPPING.

—B.B.KING

You know you've reached middle age when the morning after lasts all day.

Retirement is twice as much husband and half as much money.

How vain it is to sit down to write when you have not stood up to live.

— Henry Thoreau

Ask not for whom the dog barks. It barks for thee.

A lot of drunks only drink beer on days that end in Y.

The poor carry their burdens and the rich have them delivered.

—Neil Simon

Beware of dogs that can't hold their licker.

I live in my own little world, but it's OK…they know me here.

THERE'S A TIME TO WINK AS WELL AS TO SEE.
—BENJAMIN FRANKLIN

You'll never see a motorcycle parked outside of a psychiatrist's office.

Books are our truest form of assisted living.

Remember—the ark was built by amateurs; the Titanic by professionals.

Times change, bureaucracy lasts forever.

We read in order to know we are not alone.

—Joe Queenan

It's not how many doors you've opened for yourself, but how many you've opened for others.

Drink Coffee! Do stupid things faster with more energy.

Never drive faster than your guardian angel can fly.

There are only two distinct classes of people on this earth: those who espouse enthusiasm and those who despise it.

—Germaine de Stael

FASHION IS ABOUT WHAT YOU WEAR. STYLE IS ABOUT HOW YOU LIVE YOUR LIFE.

—RALPH LAUREN

Write it down, make it happen.

Be an idealist until the day the world is perfect.

Life ain't in holding a good hand of cards, but in playing a poor hand well.

Be an idealist until the day the world is perfect.

Stay fit. When you are 600 years old, someone may ask you to do something really big.

Wrinkles will go only where the smiles have been.

Love your enemies, for they will tell you your faults.

—Benjamin Franklin

Life does not rewind !

Perseverance: a lowly virtue whereby mediocrity achieves a glorious success.

—Ambrose Bierce

YOU'RE NEVER TOO OLD TO DO GOOFY STUFF.

Many things that cannot be overcome when they are together, yield themselves up when taken little by little.

—Plutarch

He's a fool that makes his doctor his heir.

—Benjamin Franklin

Beating your head against a wall is more likely to produce a concussion in the head than a hole in the wall.

Oh please keep us alive. There are ten for dinner, and food for five.

MONDAY is a four-letter word.

The pleasure we derive from doing favors is partly in the feeling it gives us that we are not altogether worthless.

You can't be depressed now; the worst is yet to come.

——Molly Ivins

A mob is not a crowd.

Most people hurry after pleasure so fast that they rush right past it.

LOVE IS BEING STUPID TOGETHER.

It's OK to be lost, just be sure you're making good time.

Raising a teenager is like nailing Jell-O to a tree.

They say that in the end truth will triumph, but it's a lie.

—Anton Chekov

Just be happy that your enemies are not twins.

Love make's the world go 'round, but it's laughter that keeps us from getting dizzy.

Only hang out with people who make you look good.

Build something that is idiot proof and someone will make a better idiot.

It's hard to fight when you're holding hands.

Most of us have two kinds of people in our lives—those whom we keep waiting and those for whom we are willing to wait.

PLAY IT FOR LAUGHS !

Snowflakes are one of nature's most fragile things, but just look what they can do when they stick together.

Learn to speak loving words —nobody resents them.

You don't need to have company to dinner to use the best china.

For every minute you are angry, you lose sixty seconds of happiness.

Where's there's marriage without love, there will *be* love without marriage.

—Benjamin Franklin

Love your enemies. It sure as hell will make them feel foolish.

If vegetarians eat vegetables, what do humanitarians eat?

Depression—anger without enthusiasm.

A kiss can be a comma, a question mark or an exclamation point.

IT COSTS NOTHING TO SMILE.

A memorandum is written not to inform the reader but to protect the writer.
—Dean Acheson

Everybody does better when everybody does better.

Old songs are little houses in which our hearts once lived.
—Ben Hecht

Writing legitimizes daydreaming. —Christine Schwartz

A true friend remembers your birthday; just not which one.

We draw our strength from the very despair in which we have been forced to live.

—Cesar Chavez

Most folks remember a kind deed…especially if they did it.

Do you prefer to be the statue or the bird?

Don't compare yourself to others; they are more screwed up than you are.

FOLLOW YOUR INNER MOONLIGHT!

He who does not enjoy his own company is usually right.

—Coco Chanel

SIMPLIFY ! SIMPLIFY !

You can't depend on your eyes when your imagination is out of focus.

—Mark Twain

Wildness is the preservation of the world. —Thoreau

A stressed out pretty girl may be suffering from a acute anxiety.

Beautiful young people are accidents of nature but beautiful old people are works of art.

—Eleanor Roosevelt

We aim above the mark to hit the mark.

—Ralph Waldo Emerson

A room without books is like a body without a soul.

—Cicero

When guests stay too long, treat them like family members. If they don't leave then, they never will.

GET USED TO THE FAILINGS OF THOSE AROUND YOU.

It's not enough to be right. You have to avoid the Appearance of being wrong.
—Bill Dougherty

An advanced old woman is uncontrollable by any earthly force.
—Dorothy Sayers

Don't sweat the petty things and don't pet the sweaty things.

Laughter is the shortest distance between two people.

If you have to eat crow, eat it while it is young and tender.
—Bob Newstead

We can't all be heroes because somebody has to sit on the curb and clap as they go by.

—Will Rogers

Make the most of yourself, for that is all there is of you.

— Ralph W. Emerson

A kiss may not be the truth; but it's what we want it to be.

—Steve Martin

Some male managers think nine women should be able to produce a child in one month.

LET'S HAVE SOME FUN! WHEN YOU'RE DEAD— YOU'RE DONE.

In the 60s people took acid to make the world weird. Now the world is weird and people take Prozac to make it normal.

Too many drinks just may cause you to think you can sing.

We don't learn from our mistakes as much as we learn by getting caught at them.

Distinguish people of words from people of deeds.

Never let things be seen when they're only half-finished.

Most people don't know what they're doing, and a lot of them are very good at it.

If a gal can't be skinny, at least let her friends be fat.

What a relief to wake up very early on a cold morning to find that it's sleep-late Sunday.

BE LUCKY; GO HAPPY !

Anyone born in America can become president; it's a risk you have to take.

It's OK to put your best foot forward—just watch where you step.

Nurture bacteria. It's the only culture some people have.

Not all who wander are lost.

In the cookies of life friends are the chocolate chips.

Stand up. Keep fighting! —Paul Wellstone

Humpty Dumpty was pushed.

Do not tiptoe through life only to arrive safely at death.

BE THE CHANGE YOU WISH TO SEE IN THE WORLD.

The greatness of a nation and its moral progress can be judged by the way its animals are treated.

—M. Gandhi

Ignore your rights and they'll go away.

It's not necessary to kill someone in order to read an obituary with pleasure.

Panic NOW — avoid the rush.

Did you ever stop to think and forget to start?

Some cause happiness wherever they go; others
whenever they go.
— Oscar Wilde

Thank you for not being perky !

40% of all statistics are wrong.

Music is the shorthand of emotion. Music be the food of
love, play on.
— Shakespeare

FAIRY TALES DO COME TRUE.

Growing older is mandatory. Growing UP
is optional.

Live by the sun, Love by the moon.

If you think someone has a lot more depth than
appears on the surface; consider—deep down, he's
shallow.
                                        —Peter DeVries

Give a weed an inch and it will take a yard.

Good things happen over coffee.

Inside us lives a skinny woman crying to get
out. But we can usually shut the bitch up with
cookies.

He has all the virtues I dislike and none of the
vices I admire.
                                        —Winston Churchill

Eat, drink and be merry.

So many people with the gift of gab never wrap it up.

TO PLAY MUSIC LIKE AN ANGEL BE ONE.

Dress reality in the colors of your
dreams.
                              —Nina Ricci

If all the world's a stage, I want better lighting.

I didn't attend the funeral, but I sent a nice letter
saying I approved of it.
                              —Mark Twain

Refuse to be ordinary !

If you can't be a good example — then, you'll just have to be a horrible warning.

He has no enemies, but is intensely disliked by his friends.

—Oscar Wilde

All you need is love. —The Beatles

Have no job. Have no money. Have no car. But *can* whistle.

YOUTH HAS NO AGE.   —PICASSO

Life is like a piano, what you get out of it depends on how you play it.

Laughing is like jogging on the inside.

A man's got to do what a man's got to do. A woman

must do what he can't.

—Rhonda Hansome

If they don't have chocolate in heaven, don't go.

Every time I close the door on reality, it comes in through the windows.

The phrase "working mother" is redundant.

—Jane Sellman

The person who makes you angry controls you.

Thirty-five is when you finally get your head together and your body starts falling apart.

—Caryn Leschen

CHOOSE TO BE HAPPY !

I'm not offended by all the dumb blonde jokes because I know I'm not dumb—and I'm also not blonde.

—Dolly Parton

Wisdom comes with age, but then again, sometimes age comes alone.

If high heels were so wonderful, men would still be wearing them.

--Sue Grafton

Families are like fudge...mostly sweet, with a few nuts.

When women are depressed they either eat or go shopping. Men invade another country.

—Elayne Boosler

Good quality lies don't contradict the truth; they improve it.

A pretty girl is like a melody; but too many guys

don't know how to carry a tune.

It's easy to forgive and forget—just not at the same time.

When you fall down, you may as well figure out what else you can do while you're down there.

YOU JUST CAN'T REPAIR STUPID.

You're getting old when you get the same sensation from a rocking chair that you once got from a roller coaster.

We have only one person to blame, and that's each other.

—Barry Beck

It's frustrating when you know all the answers but nobody bothers to ask you the questions.

Today's mighty oak is just yesterday's nut that held its ground.

Lord, keep your arm around my shoulder and your hand over my mouth.

The game of life is won by inches. Be a little faster, a little smarter, a little better.

It is better to fail in originality than to succeed in imitation.

—Herman Melville

To understand is not to excuse; just as to forgive is not to forget.

You never get a second chance to make a first impression.

—Will Rogers

THE SECRET OF SUCCESS IS TO KNOW
SOMETHING NOBODY ELSE KNOWS.
                    —ARISTOTLE ONASSIS

There are two kinds of people, those
who do the work and those who take the
credit. Try to be in the first group;
there is less competition there.
                    —Indira Gandhi

A mother's love is a twinkle in her eye, her heart's pitty-pat,
her star in the sky.

You define a good plane ride by negatives— You
didn't get hijacked, you didn't crash, you didn't throw
up, and you weren't late. So you're grateful.
                    —Paul Theroux

Laughter is our instant vacation.

Because we don't care doesn't mean we don't understand.

Economy is going without something you do want
in case you should some day want something you
probably won't want.

—Anthony Hope

Keep your best friend, that person knows too
much about you.

*My opinion may have changed but not the
fact that I am right.*

When life gives you lemons, ask for a bottle of tequila
and some salt.

YIELD TO TEMPTATION, IT MAY NOT PASS YOUR
WAY AGAIN.

Eat to please yourself, but dress to
please others.

—Ben Franklin

SMIRK

A good plan today is better than a perfect plan tomorrow.

Shoot for the moon; even if you miss you'll land among the stars.

The mind doesn't knows what the tongue wants.

Recipe for a full life: Love, laughter and red lipstick.

It's always cocktail hour in some time zone, somewhere.

If she were a bear people would think it natural for her to have hairy legs, excess body fat and to wake up growling.

If it's the last dance, dance backwards!

Most women can do anything if they have the right shoes.

GO CONFIDENTLY IN THE DIRECTION OF YOUR DREAMS.

Good friends are cheaper than a shrink. Here's to good friends !

Normal is just a setting on the washing machine.

A baby is a small member of the family that makes love stronger, days shorter, nights longer, the home happier, clothes shabbier, the past forgotten and the future worth living for.

Be sure to live happily ever after.

People who are the happiest don't have the best of everything. They make the best of everything they have.

Who were you before you put yourself last?

Try a little more laughter, a little less worry, a little more kindness, and a little less hurry.

Spoil yourself.

Grandparents sprinkle stardust over the lives of little children.

IT'S NOT SHOPPING— IT'S RETAIL THERAPY.

Today will be a good day. Somehow!

Avoid biting when a simple growl will do.

If you have faith no bigger even than a mustard seed... nothing will prove impossible to you.
                                        —Matthew 17:20

You gotta have heart —miles and miles of heart.

Life is like a roll of toilet paper. The closer it gets to the end, the faster it goes.

How would things be today if Indians had strip-searched the Puritans?

A smile is an inexpensive way to improve your looks.

A fat stomach never breeds fine thoughts.
—St. Jerome

A good face, they say, is a letter of recommendation.
—Henry Fielding

TO IGNORE THE FACTS DOES NOT CHANGE THE FACTS.

Opportunities are never lost—someone
will take the ones you miss.

If you're in a hole—stop digging.   —Dennis Healy

Because we don't care doesn't mean we don't
understand.

The crisis of today is the joke of tomorrow.
—H G Wells

What you pawn—I will redeem. — Sherman Alexie

Mistakes are a fact of life. It is the response to errors
that counts.
—Nikki Giovanni

Nature gives you the face you have at 20; it's up
to you to merit the face you have at 50.
——Coco Chanel

Never go to a doctor whose office plants have died.

—Erma Bombeck

For everything there is a season, and a time forever matter under heaven.

—Ecclesiastes 3:1

THE BALLOT IS STRONGER THAN THE BULLET.
—ABRAHAM LINCOLN

You are never too old to become younger.

—Mae West

Anything one man can imagine, other men can make real.
—Jules Verne

I exercise every morning without fail. One eyelid goes up and the other follows.
—Pete Postlethwaite

Exercise is labor without weariness. —Samuel Johnson

The conception of two people living together for 25 years without having a cross word suggests a lack of spirit only to be admired in sheep.

—Alan Patrick Herbert

Hours fly, flowers die, new days, new ways pass by.
Love stays.

Merlot makes us think silly things
Bordeaux makes us say them
Champagne makes us do them.

Tell me, where is this bright side you speak of?

I've found that the best way to give advice to my children is to find out what they want to do and then advise them to do it.

—Harry S. Truman

TO FIND TRUE HAPPINESS: REMINISCE.

—CASANOVA

Being good as a son and obedient as a young man is, perhaps, the root of a man's character.

—Confucius

A true friend never gets in your way unless you happen to be going down.

—Arnold Glasgow

Hard work spotlights the character of people: Some turn up their sleeves, some turn up their noses, and some don't turn up at all.

—Sam Ewing

People forget how fast you did a job—but they remember how well you did it.

—Howard Newton

The man who views the world at 50 the same as he did at 20 has wasted 30 years of his life.

—Muhammad Ali

Life is like a game of cards. The hand you are dealt is determinism; the way you play it is free will.

—Jawaharlal Nehru

The longer I live, the more beautiful life becomes.

—Frank Lloyd Wright

Passion makes the world a limitless place.

It is very difficult to be mad at someone who makes you laugh.

—Les Parrott, Ph. D

MAINTAIN A CLEAN KITCHEN—DINE OUT.

The best way to make sure you are removing a weed and not a precious plant is to pull on it. If it comes out easily, it is a precious plant.

Whenever I feel blue, I start to breathe again.

The easiest way to find something lost around the house is to buy a replacement.

A smile is a curve that sets everything straight.
—Phyllis Diller

To me, old age is always 15 years older than I am.
—Bernard Baruch

Whether you think you can, or think you can't, you're right.
—Henry Ford

A career is a series of comebacks. —Ricky Nelson

If you want to be different, you got to DO something different.

—Ellis Marsalis

Love is or it ain't. —Toni Morrison

Youth looks ahead, old age looks back, and middle age looks tired.

—Debbie Hansen

MONEY, LIKE WATER, WILL ALWAYS FIND AN OUTLET.

```
Treat the earth well: it was not given
to you by your parents, it was loaned
to you by your children.
```

Privacy is something you can sell, but you can't buy it back.

—Bob Dylan

A man's friendships are one of the best measures of his worth.

—Charles Darwin

Family reunions aren't usually catered.

Blessed are the flexible, for they shall not get bent out of shape.

Keep going. There's a lot of good stuff out there.

—James Earl Jones

It is bad to suppress laughter. It goes back down and spreads your hips.

—Fred Allen

Men hate those to whom they have lied.

—Victor Hugo

Everyone says forgiveness is a lovely idea, until they have something to forgive.
>   —C.S. Lewis

TIME IS THE LENS THROUGH WHICH DREAMS ARE CAPTURED.
>   –FRANCIS FORD COPPOLA

Plan. You must know where you're going so you know when you've arrived.

To understand is not to excuse; just as to forgive is not to forget.

Cherish your visions and dreams—they are the children of your soul.

One needn't study to become a fool.   —Mexican proverb

Attention Teenagers: "NO" is a complete sentence!

The absence of alternatives clears the mind marvelously.

—Henry Kissinger

Knowledge speaks but wisdom listens.

Begin now. If not now; when?   —Goethe

Many of us have a kitchen only because it came with the house.

WHY NOT ME ?

To the world you might be one person, but to one person you might be the world.

In debt? Throw the bills on the ground, the dust will settle them.

If the definition of beautiful gets any thinner, no one will fit.

Speak your mind even if your voice shakes.
—Maggie Kuhn

First they ignore you. Then they laugh at you. Then they fight you. Then you win.
—M.Ghandi

May you grow old on one pillow.
—Armenian Wedding Blessing

Love is sweet, but it's nice to have bread with it.
—Yiddish proverb

Go confidently into the direction of your dreams !

Hold your forked tongue and offer a silver-spoon tongue.
—Gilda Carle, Ph. D.

ONLY THE KNIFE KNOWS WHAT GOES ON IN THE
HEART OF A PUMPKIN.

Promises and piecrusts are made to be
broken.
—Jonathan Swift

Pain has its reasons, pleasure is totally indifferent.

The secret of neurosis is to be found in the family
battle of wills to see who can refuse longest to help
with the dishes.

Be naughty! Save Santa the trip.

Freedom of choice is a universal principle to which there
should be no exceptions.
—Mikhail Gorbachev

Choose a job you love, and you will never have to work a day in your life.

—Confucious

Why is it called tourist season if we can't shoot them?

If you break it you buy it, you either own it or you fix it.

How can a person be so thirsty in the morning when he drank so much the night before?

NO HOME IS COMPLETE WITHOUT DOG AND/OR CAT HAIR.

Asking a question is embarrassing for a moment, but not asking is embarrassing for a lifetime.

—Haruki Murakami

Never take life seriously. Nobody gets out alive anyway.

Every man wants a wife who is beautiful, understanding, economical, and a good cook; but unfortunately, the law allows only one wife.

Always get the last word in: Apologize.

If you do your holiday shopping at the 7-Eleven store, you know you have a problem.

Where the Press is free and every man able to read all is safe.

—Thomas Jefferson

Keep it simple. Let's do the obvious thing—the common thing—but let's do it uncommonly well.

—Leo Burentt

Age is a very high price to pay for maturity.

Why eat a lot of natural foods considering that most people die of natural causes?

IF AT FIRST YOU DON'T SUCCEED––DUCT TAPE.

The real price of everything is the toil and trouble of acquiring it.
—Adam Smith

There are two kinds of pedestrians — the quick and the dead.

If quitters never win, and winners never quit, then who is the fool who said, "Quit while you're ahead?"

It is easier to get forgiveness than permission.

Good Health is merely the slowest possible rate at which one can die.

Some people are like Slinkies, not really good for anything, but you still can't help but smile when you see one tumble down the stairs.

All of us could take a lesson from the weather. It pays no attention to criticism.

The only difference between a rut and a grave is the depth.

How is it one careless match can start a forest fire, but it takes a whole box to start a campfire?

BILLS TRAVEL THROUGH THE MAIL AT TWICE THE SPEED OF CHECKS.

If you must choose between two evils, pick the one you've never tried before.

For every action there is an equal and opposite government program.

Always acknowledge a fault. This will throw those in authority off their guard and give you an opportunity to commit more.

Opportunities always look bigger going than coming.
—Mark Twain

If you look like your passport picture, you probably need the trip.

No husband has ever been shot while doing the dishes.

Middle age is when broadness of the mind and narrowness of the waist change places.

If you're too open-minded, your brains will fall out.

Junk is something you've kept for years and throw away three weeks before you need it.

THE ONLY TIME YOU CAN'T AFFORD TO FAIL IS THE LAST TIME YOU TRY.
                              —CHARLES KETTERING

Experience is a wonderful thing. It enables you to recognize a mistake when you make it again.

Anyone who thinks logically provides a nice contrast to the real world.

Blessed are they who can laugh at themselves for they shall never cease to be amused.

The great gift of the human imagination is that it has no limits or ending.

Worry is the interest you pay on trouble before it comes.

Just because you're paranoid doesn't mean you are crazy.

—Lenny Bruce

It costs nothing to buy a dream ...and it is the best investment you can make.

—Dr. Robert Schuller

Imagination is the preview of life's coming attractions.

—Larry Eisenberg

Happiness is not a horse; you cannot harness it.

—Russian proverb

IF YOU'RE GOING TO GET OLD, YOU MIGHT AS
WELL GET AS OLD AS YOU CAN.

There are worse crimes than burning
books. One is not reading them.
—Joseph Brodsky

A truly happy person is one who can enjoy the
scenery on a detour.

Just when the caterpillar thought the world was over, it
became a butterfly.

Life isn't about finding yourself. Life is about creating
yourself.

Business is a dog-eat-dog world. Politics is the exact
opposite.

—NYC Mayor Michael Bloomberg

A book is like a garden carried in the pocket.

—Chinese proverb

One of life's mysteries is how a 2-pound box of candy can make a person gain 5 pounds.

Baroque—when you're out of Monet.

The nice part about living in a small town is that when you don't know what you're doing, someone else does.

A BIRD DOES NOT SING BECAUSE IT HAS AN ANSWER. IT SINGS BECAUSE IT HAS A SONG.

What if it truly doesn't matter what you do but how you do whatever you do? How would this change what you choose to do?

Ideas are to literature what light is to painting.

—Paul Bourget

We don't stop playing because we grow old; we grow old because we stop playing.

—George Bernard Shaw

Who's in debt? It's simply a negative cash flow.

In literature, as in love, is we are astounded by what chosen by others.

—Andre Maurois

Coffee should be black as hell, strong as death, and sweet as love.

Silences make the real conversation between friends. Not the saying but the never needing to say is what counts.

——Margaret Lee Runbeck

Do justice, love kindness and walk humbly with your dog.

Some people have an abiding sense of tragedy that sustains them through temporary periods of joy.

HEY, IT'S ONLY A GAME !

The measure of love is to love without measure.

After all...tomorrow is another day.   —Scarlett O'Hara

Diplomacy is telling a man to go to hell so that he looks forward to making the trip.

I believe in looking reality straight in the eye and denying it.
—Garrison Keillor

Courage is a spelling bee, and your word is superciliousness. Courage is tasting the vegetable before making a face.

Courage is sometimes having to say good-bye.

Every branch blossoms according to the root from which it sprung.

Figures lie and liars figure.

If you can't be kind, at least have the decency to be vague.

Men seldom make passes at girls who wear glasses.
—Dorothy Parker

SOME MISTAKES ARE TOO MUCH FUN TO ONLY MAKE ONCE.

If you lend someone $20, and never see that person again, it was probably worth it.

Birthdays are good for you; the more you have, the longer you live.

The election ballot—a love song to your country.

We could learn a lot from crayons: some are sharp, some pretty, some dull, some have weird names, and all are different colors but they all have learned to live in the same box.

Avoid temptation. Unless, of course, you can't resist it.

Appalachia is so far behind the times that it has to push the moonshine out in order to let the sunshine in.

Plough deep while sluggards sleep, and you shall have corn to sell and to keep.

—Poor Richard

When a thief kisses you, count your teeth.

To learn more and more about less and less, until
eventually we shall know everything about nothing.
—Motto "Boneheads Club"

WHERE IGNORANCE IS BLISS IT'S FOLLY TO BE
WISE.

Everybody wants to save the Earth;
nobody wants to help Mom with the
dishes.
—P.J.O'Rourke

For every human problem, there is a neat, simple solution
and it is always wrong.
—H. L. Menken

Dear I. R. S.: I would like to cancel my subscription—
please remove my name from your mailing list.

If you're smoking here you'd better be on fire.

If you've done well in life it's your responsibility to send the elevator back down for the next guy.

—Jack Lemmon

If you are what you eat, I want to be chocolate cake and champagne.

Many are young at heart; but their other parts slightly older.

You only fail when you quit.

— Mark Gumz,

If life gives you lemons, make lemonade. If life gives you limes, make margaritas.

IF IT'S STUPID BUT IT WORKS, IT ISN'T STUPID.

Friends make sure you don't get too comfortable and fall asleep and miss your life.

Would it have killed some of those martyrs to have left a suicide note?

He could overcome his gambling addiction if he just played his cards right.

There was total darkness as far as the eye could see.

He worked like a fiend in his campaign against satanic cults.

The assassin bought a gun and silencer with all the bells and whistles.

Introducing a tax on junk food is the government's one-size-fits-all solution to the obesity epidemic.

I swear to God, I'm agnostic!

Just like the rest of his generation, he marched to a different drummer.

JOY TO THE WORLD. JOY TO YOU AND ME.

Some people will believe in global warming when hell finally freezes over.

Next time you think you're perfect, try walking on water.

Many of life's failures are people who did not realize how close they were to success when they gave up.
— Edison

He was so angry about the cloning issue that he was beside himself.

Some of us have tried relaxing, but feel more comfortable being tense.

Some university graduates are prime examples of that modern innovation: the pedigreed simpleton.

Never put off until tomorrow what you can avoid altogether.

Where do things go when they are lost?
—George Carlin

Since everything is in our heads, we had better not lose them.

—Coco Chanel

ANGELS FLY BECAUSE THEY TAKE THEMSELVES LIGHTLY.

We know nothing of tomorrow; our
business is to be good and happy today.
                        —Sydney Smith

Self-love is not so vile a sin as self-neglecting.
                        —William Shakespeare

If you aren't up to a little magic occasionally, you
should not attempt to cook.
                        —Colette

They never use the word "alleged" in sports reporting,
only in political news.

Excuses are not worth the time they take and apologies are
useless. Friendship is true, just read between the lines.

Teenagers are too old to do the stuff kids do and not
old enough to do things adults do, so they do things
nobody else does.

If you shoot a mime, should you use a silencer?

—Steven Wright

Let me tell you, you couldn't pay me to be twenty again.

Life is what happens to you when you are making other plans.

—John Lennon

EVERYTHING I SAY IS FULLY SUBSTANTIATED BY MY OWN OPINION.

Do you ever wonder if illiterate people get the full effect of alphabet soup?

The big print giveth and the small print taketh away.

—Bishop Fulton J. Sheen

There has been only one indispensable man in the history of the world. His name was Adam.

—Leo Burnett

Just remember, once you're over the hill, you begin to pick up speed.

—Charles Schulz

Bankruptcy is a proceeding in which you put your money in your pants pocket and give your coat to your creditors.

—Joey Adams

The power of accurate observation is commonly call cynicism by those who have not got it.

—George Bernard Shaw

Indians never get lost—although sometimes the path wanders.

There's always one fox that thinks burrowing should be abandoned because it makes life so hard on the hounds.

WHAT THIS COUNTRY NEEDS IS MORE UNEMPLOYED POLITICIANS.

We often don't put our money where our mouth is because our feet are often already there.

If people don't want to come out to the ballpark, nobody's going to stop them.

—Yogi Berra

A good lawyer knows the law. A great lawyer knows the judge.

Cats are like women and women are like cats—they are both very ungrateful.

—Damon Runyon

A man is not honest simply because he has not had a chance to steal.

—Jewish proverb

There are days when it takes all you've got just to keep up with the losers.

Things to do today: #1 Get up, #2 Survive, #3 Go back to bed.

Never let them see you sweat.

Doesn't expecting the unexpected make the unexpected the expected?

A TRUE FRIEND STABS YOU IN THE FRONT.
—OSCAR WILDE

An idea isn't responsible for the people who believe in it.
—Don Marquis

I'm trying to arrange my life so that I don't have to be present.

The difference between genius and stupidity is that genius has its limits.

I talk to myself because I like dealing with a better class of people.

Ask a kid to take a bath. " May I take it to a movie?" he may ask.

When a man opens the car door for his wife, probably either the car is new or the wife is.

Old friends are best—they know everything about you but can't remember it.

Life is too short to cook for strangers.

If Patrick Henry thought taxation without representation was bad, he should see it with representation.

STAY WITH US. THERE'S MORE TO COME.
—NATIONAL PUBLIC RADIO

If truth is beauty why not get your hair styled at the library?

An arch is two weaknesses, which together make a strength.
—Leonardo da Vinci

How can you be out of money when you still have more checks?

I'm confused—wait. . .maybe I'm not.

Having critics praise you is like having the hangman say you have a pretty neck.
—Eli Wallach

Some countries say they have no crime. "We have the police and the army to do that for us," they say.

What we need is a sport that is suited to those talented in pacing back and forth and worrying.
>   —Raymond Lesser

Love is like war: easy to begin but very hard to stop.
>   —H.L. Mencken

A KID KNOWS HE'S UNLOVED WHEN HIS PARENTS PAY HIS ALLOWANCE IN TRAVELERS' CHECKS.

You grow up the day you have your first real laugh at yourself.
>   —Ethel Barrymore

The dining table is a date with love and friendship.

—Colette

If God had intended man to engage in strenuous sports, He would have given us better knees.

—Dr. Robert Ray

Stay young, you'll live longer.

Television is an invention that permits you to be entertained in your living room by people you wouldn't have in your home.

—David Frost

Everything we do in life is based on fear, especially love.

——Mel Brooks

The bravest thing that men do is to love women.

—Mort Sahl

I believe every human has a finite number of heartbeats. I don't intend to waste any of mine running around doing exercise.

—Neil Armstrong

NOTHING IS REALLY REAL UNLESS IT HAPPENS ON TELEVISION.

–DANIEL J. BOORSTIN

There's a five-day waiting period for buying a gun. Why don't they have the same for haircuts?

He hasn't an enemy in the world—but all his friends hate him.

—Eddie Cantor

You can tell a lot about a person by the way he/she handles (a) a rainy day, (b) lost luggage, and (c) tangled Christmas tree lights.

Disraeli is a self-made man who worships his creator.

—John Bright

He can compress the most words into the smallest ideas of any man I have ever met.

—AbrahamLincoln

He doesn't know the meaning of the word fear; but then again he doesn't know the meaning of most words.

Everything that lives and endures for more than a day after we die is eternal.

—Yehuda Amichai

Never raise your hand to your children; it leaves your midsection unprotected.

—Robert Orben

LET'S NOT SPOIL THIS WITH WORDS.

Some people used to think Hollywood was fast women and fast cars, but it's really just fast food.

Legs are the wheels of thought. —E. Augier

To feel at home, stay at home. A foreign country is not designed to make you comfortable. It's designed to make its own people comfortable.

—Clifton Fadiman

One swell thing about the U.S.A. is that newspapers can print whatever stories they want. Another one is that nobody has to read them.

—Dave Barry

The moment of waking up is the riskiest moment of the day. ...after that take heart of grace for the rest of the day.

—Franz Kafka

Youth condemns; maturity condones.

—Amy Lowell

...the kind of guy who, if you were drowning 20 feet from shore, would throw you a 15-foot rope.

—Eugene McCarthy

FORBIDDEN FRUIT HAS MADE FOR MANY A BAD JAM.

No animal should ever jump up on the dining-room furniture unless absolutely certain that he can hold his own in the conversation.

—Fran Lebowitz

Life may not be the party we hoped for...but while we are here we might as well dance.

Cats are smarter than dogs. You can't get eight cats to pull a sled through the snow.

—Jeff Valdez

Is not the whole world a vast house of assignation in which the filing system has been lost?

—Quintin Crisp

Heredity means you blame your parents, not yourself.

When you play country music backwards do your wife, dog and job all come back to you?

There are parts of Wales where the only concession to gaiety is a striped shroud.

—Gwyn Thomas

Predictions are hard, especially about the future.

—Yogi Bera

Those who cannot remember the mistakes of the past are doomed to repeat them.

—George Santayana

ILLITERATE? WRITE FOR HELP.

It's not fair to take on a battle of wits with an unarmed person.

Recipes are a guide from which you cook your own way.

The internet is like a herd of performing elephants with diarrhea—massive, difficult to redirect, awe-inspiring and a source of a mind-boggling amount of excrement.

—Gene Spofford

If you're not outraged; you're not paying attention.

Everything comes to him who hustles while he waits.

—Thomas Edison

There are two ways to find out if you're still alive. One is to feel your pulse, the other—see if you're having a fight with somebody.

—Tom Wolfe

Have you noticed that anyone driving slower than you is always an idiot?

—George Carlin

Mom said it's not bragging if it's true.

Be sure you know words small enough for friends to understand you.

WE MAY HAVE OUR FAULTS, BUT BEING WRONG ISN'T ONE OF THEM.

Fashion can be bought. Style one must possess.

—Edna W. Chase

Progress might have been all right once, but it has gone on too long.

—Ogden Nash

You can't wait for inspiration. You have to go after it with a club.

—Jack London

Oh, the things you can think!

—The Cat in the Hat

A real friend is one who walks in when the rest of the world walks out.

The amount you talk about your troubles is in inverse relation to how many people who are willing to listen to you.

When people agree with me, I always feel that I must be wrong.

—Oscar Wilde

Frogs are lucky. They can eat what bugs them.

The English language is the sea which receives tributaries from every region under heaven.

—Ralph W. Emerson

A JOCKEY IS ONLY AS GOOD AS HIS HORSE.

Each of us carries a room within
ourselves, waiting to be furnished and
peopled.
                              —Susan Sontag

Chocolate and shoes take away the blues.

If people never did silly things, nothing intelligent
would ever get done.
                              —Ludwig Wittgenstein

What wine goes with vodka?

I've given my memoirs far more thought than any of my
marriages. You can't divorce a book.
                              —Gloria Swanson

All the fun's in how you say a thing. —Robert Frost

You need a new mirror when you see someone there who reminds you of an older brother.

Be yourself—who is better qualified?
—Frank Giblin

The quickest way to double your money is to fold it and put it back in your pocket.
—Will Rogers

VISION IS THE ART OF SEEING THINGS INVISIBLE.
—JONATHAN SWIFT

Over 25% of human genes are the same as those of a banana. Why should we take ourselves so seriously?

Everest isn't a very hard mountain. It's just a little bit too high.
—A mountain climber

A country without its czar is like a village without an idiot.

—Russian proverb

It takes about ten years to get used to how old you are.

Subway riders fantasize that loud talkers would be seated next to anyone who is snoring.

Cabbage: a vegetable about as large and wise as a man's head.

—Ambrose Bierce

Cowboys are like the weather—nothing can be done to change them.

Never play leapfrog with a unicorn.

One reason I don't drink is that I want to know when I am having a good time.

—Lady Nancy Astor

I DON'T CARE WHAT IS WRITTEN ABOUT ME SO LONG AS IT ISN'T TRUE.

–DOROTHY PARKER

A man is never drunk if he can lay on the floor without holding on.

—Joe E. Lewis

Whoever said money can't buy happiness didn't know where to shop.

Premarital sex slowly evolves into premarital sox.

The nice thing about egotists is that they don't talk about other people.

—Lucille S. Harper

The most important thing in a relationship between a man and a woman is that one of them be good at taking orders.

—Linda Festa

Lettin' the cat outta the bag is a whole lot easier'n puttin' it back.

—— Will Rogers

I don't know anything about music. In my line you don't have to.

—Elvis Presley

Mirror, mirror on the wall...what the #!&@$ happened?

SOME PEOPLE ARE NEIGHBORS IN ZIP CODE ONLY.

When you are eight years old, nothing is any of your business.

—Lenny Bruce

Hell is full of musical amateurs. --George Bernard Shaw

Small villages need their freaks, goofballs, pinheads, schizophrenics, adulterers, freckled children, Peeping Toms and has-beens in order to feel like we all lived upstanding, fulfilled, committed lives.
                                        ---Kurst Rheinheimer

A gentleman is a man who can play the accordion but doesn't.

Never invest in anything that eats or needs repairing.
                                        —Billy Rose

The secret of staying young is to live honestly, eat slowly, and lie about your age.
                                        —Lucille Ball

California is a great place to live if you're an orange.

The worst part of success is trying to find someone who is happy for you.

—Bette Midler

When you have eliminated the impossible, whatever remains, however improbable, must be the truth.

— Sherlock Holmes

IF I ONLY HAD A LITTLE HUMILITY, I'D BE PERFECT.

—TED TURNER

Loneliness is like a hammer blow that shatters glass but hardens steel.

—Fania Klausner

The easiest way to be good at golf is to be bad at arithmetic.

His lack of education is more than compensated for by his keenly developed moral bankruptcy.

—Woody Allen

A candle is not dimmed by lighting another candle.

By the way, childhood does come with an expiration date.

Every clown has a silver lining.

Don't look at the numbers, don't look in the mirror. Never retire and never die.
—Arthur Laurents.

Trust everybody—but do cut the cards.
—Finley P. Dunne

See what others merely observe.   —Sherlock Holmes

THE CURE FOR BOREDOM IS CURIOSITY. THERE IS NO CURE FOR CURIOSITY.
—ELLEN PARR.

A bore is a man who, when you ask him how he is, tells you.

—Bert Leston Taylor

You don't stop laughing because you grow old. You grow old because you stop laughing.

—Michael Pritchard

It's not whether you get knocked down; it's whether you get up.

—Vince Lombardi

We're FINE: Fouled up, Insecure, Neurotic, Egomaniac.

You cannot shake hands with a clenched fist.

—Golda Meir

Flashlight: a case in which to carry dead batteries.

Money is better than poverty, if only for

financial reasons.

—*Woody Allen*

A free society is a place where it's safe to be unpopular.
—Adlai Stevenson, Jr.

NEVER UNDERESTIMATE A WOMAN'S RIGHT TO
SHOES.

Warning: The consumption of alcohol
may lead you to think that people are
laughing with you.

Remember that overnight success usually takes about fifteen
years.

—H. Jackson Browne, Jr.

Everybody can use a little digging in the dirt.
—Sue Kaylor

Hugs not drugs !

A good mystery must be good, even with the final page torn out.

—Raymond Chandler

May your joys be fat, may your troubles be lean.

A good friend will bail you out of jail. A true friend will sit next to you in jail and laugh.

——Liz Munster

A great photograph speaks to the emotions before addressing the intellect.

If in olden times the plow drew the ox in reverse position, that would explain why we now put the cart before the horse.

SHE WAS AS HELPLESS AS A BARRACUDA.

—MARY MCGRORY

While a double negative amounts to a
positive, never does a double positive
amount to a negative.

—J.L.Austin

Always approach the shrimp bowl like you own it.

One thing 'bout the ghetto, you don't have to hurry.
It'll be there tomorrow.

—Rick James

To observe that life is absurd is not an end, but a beginning.

—Albert Camus

All future and no history, all fizz and no gin.

At the top of the steeple there's only room for
one person at a time. I always meant that person
to be me.

—Robert Frost

If you can't be funny, be interesting.
—*Harold Ross*

If the unexamined life is not worth living, the unexamined past is not worth possessing.

THE WHEEL IS SPINNING BUT THE HAMSTER HAS DEPARTED.

Middle age is when you've met so many people that every new person you meet reminds you of someone else.

—Ogden Nash

Who says chocolate isn't a vegetable?

The evidence remains that the species of tree that money grows best on is, of course, the family tree.
—Brendan Gill

Be your own best friend.

If what you want is buried deep down, keep digging until you find it.

I only drink to make other people interesting
—George Jean Nathan

Art is the way we measure the health of a society.

To make an omelet—first steal an egg.
—Elmyr de Hoy

Childhood is the kingdom where nobody dies. Nobody, that matters, that is.
—Edna St. Vincent Millay

NOT ALL WILD THINGS NEED TO BE CONTROLLED AND SOMETIMES CONTROLLED THINGS NEED TO BE A LITTLE WILD.

Life's journey is not to arrive at the grave safely in a well preserved body, but rather to skid in sideways, totally worn out, shouting "wow...what a ride!"

The leaves of a tree are many but the root is one.

Pick out a star that looks good and follow it.
—Garrison Keillor

It's pretty, but is it art?

The secret of a good speech is to have a good beginning and a good ending and to have the two as close together as possible.

She has all the qualities of leadership, except followers.
—Dennis Hastert

Don't worry about avoiding temptation; as you grow older it will avoid you.

Being a congressman feeds your vanity and starves your self-respect.
— *Lee Hamilton*

She's so blonde that even in summer she looks like a photographic negative.

MERCIFULLY NOT ALL THE STORIES THAT WE WISH TO BE TRUE ARE FALSE.

In our hearts we are all six years old. The painfulness of being rejected never grows less.
—Brendan Gill

When a country person is happy he says he can't complain.

Words of the world are the life of the world.
—Wallace Stevens

Open your heart to the possibilities.

Divas are easy to get along with once you learn to worship them.

If we don't succeed we run the risk of failure.

—Dan Quale

A house without books is like a room without windows.

——Horace Mann

No good deed goes unpunished.

One must admire a man who, even though he suspects he may be scraping the bottom of the barrel, scrapes the bottom of the barrel.

—Brendan Gill

ONCE YOU LEARN A SKILL, IT'S YOURS !

There's always a problem-solver—even if no problem has previously been seen to exist.

Let your heart see what your eyes cannot.

That we are not much sicker and much madder than we are is due exclusively to that most blessed and blessing of all natural graces—sleep.
                                        —Aldous Huxley

We're at the mercy of our own incompetence.
                                        —Daiton Rudkowski

By virtue of our all agreeing that Santa exists, we're allowed to have that joy in our lives.
                                        —Earl Dax

No job, no matter how lowly is truly "unskilled."

—Barbara Ehrenreich

Where there is no law, but every man does what is right in his own eyes, there is the least of real liberty.

—Henry M. Robert

DON'T MISS A CHANCE TO SING.

Listen to your heart and watch your dreams come true.

Go with the flow.

Never underestimate the power of chocolate.

Twenty years from now you will be more disappointed by the things you didn't do than by the things you did.

—Mark Twain

A kind heart is the most beautiful accessory.
—Stephanie Haller

If we dream only while we sleep, we're wasting half our lives.

Feeling good starts with looking good.

Trust yourself. You know more than you think you do.
—Dr. Spock

HARMONY IS SOMETHING LIKE TWO MUSICAL NOTES THAT LOVE EACH OTHER.

May you always have enough happiness to keep you sweet; enough trials to keep you strong; enough success to keep you eager; enough faith to give you courage; and enough determination to make each day a good day.

Cry and laugh less while watching television and more while watching life.

Even if you're on the right track, you'll get run over if you just sit there.

—Will Rogers

Climate is what you expect, weather is what you get.

I never give them hell. I just tell the truth and they think it's hell.

— Harry Truman

He has charm where other men have only cologne.

—Mae West

By the time you can make ends meet, they move the ends.

One hand cannot clap, it takes two.

To live well: Immerse yourself in the present moment.
—Casanova

WHAT A SORROW FOR ANYONE TO BE HIGHLY
FED AND LOWLY TAUGHT.

A bank is a place where they lend you
an umbrella in fair weather and ask for
it back when it begins to rain.
—Robert Frost

Be the CEO of your own life.

The Declaration of Independence guarantees the
American people the right to pursue happiness. You
have to catch it yourself.

Have fun !

In the entertainment industry everyone seems to get elevated to their most colorful hyperbole.

A girl must marry for love, and keep marrying until she finds it.

—Zsa Zsa Gabor

The great gift of the human imagination is that it has no limits or ending.

A hug is a great gift; one size fits all.

There is no present. There's only the immediate future and the recent past.

—George Carlin

THERE IS ALWAYS ONE MORE IMBECILE THAN YOU COUNTED ON.

Equilibrium is simply that moment when

the present is as real as the past or
the future.

—Leslie Ullman

Laughter is a universal beauty secret.

The secret of a successful party is in the greetings
and goody-byes.

—Perle Mesta

Dogs have masters, cats have staff.

If you can't run with the big dogs— stay on the porch.

The difficult we do right now; the impossible will take a
little longer.

—Seabees motto

One man that has a mind and knows it can beat ten men who haven't and don't.

—George Bernard Shaw

Never order a cocktail in a bar when you're with an empty wallet.

The two best times to plant a tree are twenty years ago and tomorrow.

—Chinese proverb

YOUR HEART'S DESIRE BE WITH YOU.

—WILLIAM SHAKESPEARE

What lies behind us and what lies before us are tiny matters compared to what lies within us.

—Oliver Wendell Holmes

If you don't talk to your cat about catnip...who will?

There are two chance to find out about something: slim and none.

—Dizzy Dean

Never take for granted the precious gift of hindsight.

Being married is just like any other job. It's much easier if you like the boss.

California, perpetually subdividing, perpetually suckering its dreamers.

—Joan Didion

Men show their character more clearly by what they find laughable.

I have loved the stars too fondly to be fearful of the night.

—Sarah Williams

One sees clearly only with the heart. Anything essential is invisible to the eyes.

IF ADVICE DOESN'T FIT, YOU CAN RETURN IT.

—NEIL SIMON

Never lend books, for no one ever returns them; the only books I have in my library are books that other folk have lent me.

—Anatole France

Immature artists imitate. Mature artists steal.

—Lionel Trillin

Nature, not content with denying him the ability to think, has endowed him with the ability to write.

—A.E. Housman

Glory is fleeting, but obscurity is forever.   —Napoleon

I am often asked how I got into this business. I didn't. The business got into me.

—Leo Burnett

How do you know if you've endured enough unpleasantness to deserve happiness?

May the god of your choice bless you.

If you're still trying to find yourself, maybe it's time to clean the bathroom mirror.

HE WHO RIDES A TIGER IS AFRAID TO DISMOUNT.
—CHINESE PROVERB

The significant problems we face today cannot be solved at the same level of thinking as when we created them.

—Einstein

These aren't wrinkles, they are derma-creases.

To become a great company it must to act like a great company long before it ever becomes one.

—Tom Watson, IBM

The better you get the better you better get.

—The Motley Fool

You can always recognize the pioneers by the number of arrows in their backs.

Yesterday is gone. Tomorrow has not yet come. We have only today. Let us begin.

—Mother Theresa

Tact: the art of speaking your mind in such a way that you're long gone by the time they figure out what you meant.

The gem cannot be polished without friction, nor man perfected without trials.

—Chinese Proverb

THIS ISN'T A DRESS REHEARSAL—THIS IS REAL
LIFE.

We'll never be appreciated to the
degree at which we sweat doing a job.
                        —Magda Gregory

Where words fail music speaks.

There are few hours in life more agreeable than the
hour dedicated to the ceremony known as afternoon
tea.
                        —Henry James

One can't teach a cat not to catch birds.
                        —Albert Einstein

It's a lot easier to get people to sing your praises than to
dance to your tune.

The only people who listen to both sides of an argument are the neighbors.

Garlic is the vanilla of cooking in Provence.

—French proverb

Autobiography is the last refuse of scoundrels.

—Henry Gray

I like a little rebellion now and then. It is like a storm in the atmosphere.

—Thomas Jefferson

WHEN YOU CAN'T CHANGE THE DIRECTION OF THE WIND — ADJUST YOUR SAILS.

People work longer hours so they can drive to and from work in a better car.

To travel is to discover that everyone is wrong about other countries.

—Aldous Huxley

So many women don't know how great they really are. They come to us all vogue on the outside and vague on the inside.

—Mary Kay Ash

Selling is easy if you can find someone who is buying.

—Jack Falvey

Do what you can, with what you have, where you are.

—Theodore Roosevelt

A girl whose cheeks are covered with paint has an advantage with me over one whose ain't.

—Ogden Nash

Husbands are like fires. They go out if unattended.

—Zsa Zsa Gabor

It's not money that brings happiness; it's lots of money.

> —Russian proverb

The enemy of ignorance is certainty.

Saving is a fine thing. Especially when your parents have done it for you.

> —Winston Churchill

SOME THINGS HAVE TO BE BELIEVED TO BE SEEN.

> –RALPH HODGSON

It don't mean a thing if it ain't got that swing.

> –Duke Ellington

Most people find fault like there's a reward for it.

> –Zig Ziglar

Mankind must put an end to war or war will put an end to mankind.

— John F. Kennedy

Live to love, love to live.

Again and again, step by step intuition opens the door.

— R. Buckminster Fuller

One of the oldest human needs is having someone to wonder where you are, when you don't come home at night.

— Margaret Mead

Whoever said, "It's not whether you win or lose that counts" probably lost.

— Martina Navratilova

It's a beautiful day in the neighborhood.

— Mr. Rogers

To live a life consisting only of hard work, virtue, sacrifice, and self-discipline is to be a martyr, and martyrs make lousy lovers, friends and party guests.

AT THE TOUCH OF LOVE EVERYONE BECOMES A POET.

—PLATO

If I had known I was going to live this long, I would have taken better care of myself.

— Eubie Blake

Tough times never last, tough people do.

—Robert Schuller

It is an act of courage to choose sanity and peace when others are choosing hate and war.

—San Ildefonso Pueblo

Art is the one thing separating us from bacteria.

Death is not extinguishing the light; it is putting out the lamp because the dawn has come.

—Rabindranath Tagore

The more passions and desires one has, the more ways one has of being happy.

—Charlotte-Catherine de Gramont

Some folks won't get interested in anything unless it's none of their business.

On the keyboard of life, always keep one finger on the ESCAPE key.

A positive attitude may not solve all your problems, but it will annoy enough people to make it worth the effort.

—Herm Albright

IF YOU'RE GOING TO DO SOMETHING WRONG; AT LEAST ENJOY IT !

Who cares how old you are? We want to know if you will risk looking like a fool for love, for the adventure of being alive.

Optimist: A man who gets treed by a lion but enjoys the scenery.

—Walter Winchell

Babies and young animals have the uncanny ability to turn our lives upside down.

Winning isn't everything, but wanting to is.

—Vince Lombardi

If you know the enemy and know yourself, you need not fear the result of a hundred battles.

—Sun Tzu

We may not be able to choose where we come from, but we can choose where we go from there.

A *schlemiel* spills the soup, the *schimazal* is the one it gets spilled on.

—Yiddish saying

I started out with nothing and still have most of it left.

What the world really needs is more love and less paper work.

—Pearl Bailey

THERE COMES A MOMENT WHEN YOU HAVE TO STOP REVVING UP THE CAR AND SHOVE IT INTO GEAR.

—DAVID MAHONEY

When you make your mark in the world, watch out for guys with erasers.

I have my faults. But being wrong ain't one of them.

—Jimmy Hoffa

Not only is life a bitch, it has puppies.

Time is a dressmaker specializing in alterations.

—Faith Baldwin

Too many people spend money they don't have, on things they don't need, to impress people they don't like.

You can't tell a millionaire's son from a billionaire's.

—Vance Packard

People are perfect until you fall in love with them.

Who knows what your problem is, but we'll bet it's hard to pronounce.

A VERBAL CONTRACT ISN'T WORTH THE PAPER
IT'S WRITTEN ON.

—SAMUEL GOLDWYN

If you don't own a dog...there is not
necessarily anything wrong with you,
but there may be something wrong with
your life.

—Roger Caras

If you're enough of a kid—McDonalds is a four-star
restaurant.

We could certainly slow the aging process down if it
had to work its way through Congress.

He's only a beer teetotaler, not a champagne teetotaler.

Until I was thirteen, I thought my name was "Shut Up."

— Joe Namath

Trust must be developed. You can't live comfortably in a house before it's built.

—Chun Wu

Power does not corrupt. Fear of loss of power corrupts.

—John Steinbeck

Some people are so fond of bad luck that they run half way to meet it.

We have no more right to consume happiness without producing it than to consume wealth without producing it.

PROCRASTINATION IS LIKE A CREDIT CARD; IT'S A LOT OF FUN UNTIL YOU GET THE BILL.

Why would a person take a year to write a novel when he can easily buy one for a few dollars?

—Fred Allen

Why is it easier to walk away in high heels?
—Kathleen Tessaro

If hard work is the key to success most people would rather pick the lock.

The Golden Rule is not a suggestion.

Show me someone who never gossips and I'll show you someone who isn't interested in people.

We are all born charming, fresh and spontaneous, but must learn to be civilized before we are fit for society.

You can get by on charm for about 15 minutes. After that, you'd better know something.

Everyone has a photographic memory, some just don't have film.

Politicians are all the same. They promise to build a bridge even when there is no river.

MY LUCK IS SO BAD THAT IF I BOUGHT A CEMETERY PEOPLE WOULD STOP DYING.
—ED FURGOL

Don't go around saying the world owes you a living. The world owes you nothing. It was here first.
—Mark Twain

Don't ever, ever forget how to laugh !

Although there are countless alumni of the school of hard knocks, there has yet to be a move to accredit that institution.

Many an optimist has become rich simply by buying out a pessimist.

If you're rich, you're eccentric; if you're poor, you're nuts.

—William Safire

I have a large seashell collection, which I keep scattered on beaches around the world.

—Steven Wright

One beauty of old age is that no one expects you to run into a burning building.

Humor is a way of inverting the power system.

—Don Nilsen, Arizona State U

The only thing that stops me from crying is the mascara on my eyelashes.

—Colette

IRRESPONSIBILITY IS PART OF THE PLEASURE OF ALL ART.

---JAMES JOYCE

If most auto accidents happen within five miles from home, why not move ten miles away?

We're not in Kansas anymore.

Any fool can criticize, condemn and complain—and most do.

—Dale Carnegie.

Too many silver linings contain clouds.

As long as the pleasure outweighs the pain, I'll stick with it.

—Actor, David Hyde Pierce

I'm rubber. You're glue. Whatever you say bounces off me and sticks on you.

—E.J. Montini

It is a simple plan, like a brother-in-law. However, unlike a brother-in-law, it just might work.

That rancher is all hat and no cattle.

While we can measure the temperature on Venus, we do not know what goes on inside our soufflés.
—Nicholas Kurti

BETTER THE DEVIL WE KNOW THAN THE DEVIL WE DON'T KNOW.

It was his great good fortune to live a madman and die sane.
—Miguel de Cervante

There's this lumberjack who is as tall as a six-foot tree.

He was so in love that when she spoke he heard bells; like a garbage truck backing up.

Scratch a dog and you'll find a permanent job.

You should never marry someone who doesn't make you laugh.

—Garrison Keillor

You can't perform in The Dance of Life without a really good stage!

In about 40 years we'll have thousands of old ladies bedecked with gaudy tattoos.

Support wildlife. Throw a party !

The fox that waited for the chickens to fall of their perch died of hunger.

—Greek Proverb

A MAN CHASES A WOMAN UNTIL SHE CATCHES HIM.

A wise man among the ignorant is as a beautiful girl in the company of blind men.

—Saadi

That corporation was merely a three-ring binder with a lot of debt.

Money will buy a fine dog, but only kindness will make him wag his tail.

Everyone is going to have 15 minutes of fame.

—Andy Warhol

The fruits of life fall into the hands of those who climb the tree and pick them.

—Earl Tupper, Tupperware

Kissing is a means of getting two people so close together that they can't see anything wrong with each other.

—René Yasenek

My grandmother is over eighty and still doesn't need glasses. Drinks right out of the bottle.

—Henny Youngman

If the universe is infinite, why can't we find a parking space?

There are only two ways of telling the complete truth—anonymously and posthumously.

—Thomas Sowell

HOW DO I KNOW WHAT I THINK, UNTIL I SEE WHAT I SAY?

—E.M. FOSTER

Business conventions are important in demonstrating how many people a company can operate without.

Nowadays the world is lit by lightening.

—Tennessee Williams

Nobody outside of a baby carriage or a judge's
chamber believes in an unprejudiced point of view.
—Lillian Hellman

Cork the whining!

After they have had lunch, do amphibians have to wait one
hour before getting out of the water?

Those who say that it cannot be done had better not
interrupt those already doing it.

The perfect parent is a person who has excellent
child-rearing theories and no actual child.
—Dave Berry

Baseball is 90% mental; the other half is physical.

—Yogi Bera

Life is not measured by the number of breaths we take, but by the moments that take our breath away.

REMEMBER THAT SILENCE IS SOMETIMES THE BEST ANSWER.

–DALAI LAMA

The whole value of the dime is in knowing what to do with it.

—Ralph Waldo Emerson

GET OVER IT !

Within this vale
Of toil and sin
Your head grows bald
But not your chin.

—Burma Shave

Drama is life with the dull bits cut out.

—Alfred Hitchcock

It is easier to go up into the mountains to catch tigers than to ask others for help.

—Chinese proverb

The sun looks down on nothing half so good as a household laughing together over a meal.

—C.S. Lewis

When we are happy we are always good, but when we are good we not always happy.

—Oscar Wilde

Good manners obscure many a barbarian nature.

Education appears to be the thing that enables a man to get along without using his intelligence.

—A. E. Wiggan

I KNOW SHE'S OUTSPOKEN, BUT BY WHOM?
—DOROTHY PARKER

I'm tired of all this nonsense about
beauty being only skin-deep. That's
deep enough. What do you want, an
adorable pancreas?

—Jean Kerr

Why stop to think whether this little dream might fade?

He had a photographic memory which was never developed.

You deserve a break today. —McDonald's

Do not go where the path may lead. Go instead, where there is no
path and leave a trail.

— Emerson

Dancing cheek-to-cheek is really a form of floor play.

The road to progress is always under construction.

Be not afraid. —Pope John Paul II

The lion had his mane, the peacock his gorgeous plumage, but Man finds himself in a three-button suit.

HERE COMES THE SUN !

Sometimes the bravest thing you can do is continue.

May the force be with you.   —Star Wars

Stress is when you wake up screaming and you realize you haven't gone to sleep yet.

Some lead. Some follow. Some laugh.

The law, in its awesome impartiality, gives both the rich and the poor the right to steal bread or sleep under bridges.

—Anatole France

At the end of the rainbow you'll find an empty box of crayons.

Numbers can prevaricate with a straight face what words never assume.

—P. J. O'Rourke

Here I am—now what are your other two wishes?

You gotta know when to hold 'em and know when to fold 'em.

WHERE THERE'S A WILL THERE'S RELATIVES.

It destroys one's nerves to be amiable
every day to the same human being.
                                        —Disraeli

Don't quit your day job.

Once the chess game is finished the king and the pawn
go back into the same box.

The older you get the smarter your parents seem to
become.

Life is 10% what happens to you, and 90% how you react to
it.
                                        —Lindsey

You're driving me crazy and I don't remember giving you
the keys.
                                        —Click & Clack

She has two expressions—joy and indigestion.
—Dorothy Parker

Opera is people singing when they should be talking.

Show me a nation whose national beverage is beer, and I'll show you an advanced toilet technology.
—Paul Hawkins

HE HAS EVERY ATTRIBUTE OF A DOG EXCEPT LOYALTY.
–THOMAS P. GORE

The mind is like a parachute...it only functions when open !

Old age and treachery will triumph over youth and skill.

The trouble with life in the fast lane is that you get to the other end in an awful hurry.

—John Jensen

Nothing is impossible for the man who doesn't have to do it himself.

There are two kinds of books: those that no one reads and those that no one ought to read.

—H. L. Mencken

We must believe in luck. For how else can we explain the success of those we don't like?

—John Cocteau

Never keep up with the Jonses. Drag them down to your level.

—Quentin Crisp

When in doubt, duck.   —Malcolm Forbes

If the right side of the brain controls the left side of the body does that mean that left-handed people are in their right minds?

BE BIGGER THAN THE SITUATION.

Great minds discuss ideas. Average minds discuss events. Small minds discuss people. —Eleanor Roosevelt

In a marathon you first run with your legs, then with your mind.

They're pretty happy together, but it's chemical.

Life is tough. And it's tougher if you're stupid.
—John Wayne

Some people don't know anything about computers. Not even how often to change the oil.

When you're in trouble it's good to have friends around, preferably armed.

Mothers all want their sons to grow up to be president but they don't want them to become politicians in the process.
—John F. Kennedy

Truth is more of a stranger than fiction.
—Mark Twain

Senescence begins
And middle age ends
The day your descendants
Outnumber your friends.

—Ogden Nash

RIDICULOUSNESS IS NOTHING TO BE AFRAID OF.

Be wary of a diagnosis based on X-rays that
are developed at Walgreen's.

Sharp as a tack, but also just as flat on the head.

The tongue is the only instrument that gets sharper
with use.

> — Washington Irving

Honest criticism is hard to take, particularly from a relative,
a friend, an acquaintance, or a stranger.

> —Franklin P. Jones

Suburbia is where the developer bulldozes out the
trees, then names the streets after them.

> —Bill Vaughan

A dead atheist is someone who's all dressed up
with no place to go.

> —James Duffey

The early bird catches the worm, but has a lousy social life.

Fear is being stuck in traffic when you just had two cups of coffee and a bran muffin.

YOU'RE EITHER LOST OR YOU'RE FOUND.

A happy marriage is a long conversation which always seems too short.
                                        —André Maurois

Some dieters wait to buy new clothes until they lose weight. Many are still wearing their Cub Scout uniforms.

Be wary of singing chickens and whistling women.

The two most common elements in the universe are hydrogen and stupidity.
                                        —Harlan Ellison

To succeed in the world, it is not enough to be stupid.
You must also be well-mannered.

—Voltaire

The surest sign that intelligent life exists
elsewhere in the universe is that it has never tried
to contact us.

—Bill Watterson

We didn't do anything wrong, but we won't do it again.

The secret of the demagogue is to make himself appear
as stupid as his audience so that they'll believe they're as
smart at he is.

—Karl Kraus

GENIUS MAY HAVE ITS LIMITATIONS, BUT
STUPIDITY IS NOT THUS HANDICAPPED.

—ELBERT HUBBARD

The trouble with the world is that
the stupid are cock-sure and the
intelligent are full of doubt.
                    —Bertrand Russell

If stupidity got us into this mess, then why can't it get us out?
                    —Will Rogers

It is better to keep your mouth shut and appear stupid then to open it and remove all doubt.
                    —Mark Twain

Keep on truckin'.   — Robert Crumb

What we really want is for things to remain the same but get better.
                    —Sydney J. Harris

Speak the truth, but leave immediately afterwards.
                    —Slovenian proverb

Why do drugstores make the sick walk all the way to the back of the store to get prescriptions but healthy people can buy cigarettes up front?

You get the Nobel prizes for literature, not grammar.

—Wm. Safire

He treated her like his money——took her out only when he needed something.

—Kevin Young

IT'S GREAT TO HAVE GRAY HAIR. ASK ANYONE WHO'S BALD.

There's nothing like unexpected good fortune to make a family miserable.

—Randy Cohen

Be a caterpillar by day but a butterfly by night.

—Coco Chanel

Said about a baseball manager, "He eats gunpowder every morning and washes it down with warm blood."

Nobody goes there any more, it's too crowded.

—Yogi Bera

Self-inflicted wounds are the most interesting of political mistakes.

—Jim Hoagland

Never make the same mistake twice, plenty of new ones are available.

Fashion is the healthiest motivation for losing weight.

—Karl Lagerfield

Nice guys finish last. —*Leo Durocher*

Can a book rightfully be called a book if it never gets read?

—Sherman Alexie

WHEN YOU INDULGE YOU JUST MAY BULGE.

If sex is such a natural phenomenon, how come there are so many books on how to?

—Bette Midler

The English language is truly a mongrel tongue.

When a parent gives to a child, both laugh; when a child gives to the parent, both cry.

—Yiddish proverb

When the cat and mouse agree, the grocer is ruined.

—Persian proverb

Don't piss on my legs and tell me it's raining.

—Judge Judy

At a time when everyone is abandoning ship, who remembers to bring the oars?

People who love sausage and respect the law should never watch either being made.

—Otto vonBismarck

Do one outrageous, annoying thing a day, then run like hell.

With cats, some way, one rule is true, don't speak until you are spoken to.

—T.S. Elliot

THE STONE AGE DID NOT END FOR LACK OF STONE.

—SHEIK ZAKI YAMANI

If at first you don't succeed, skydiving
is not for you.

Some of us dream in color but live in black and white.

I gave an order to the cat, and the cat gave it to its tail.
—Chinese proverb

Life is a journey not a destination.

Never underestimate the power of very stupid people in
large groups.
—John Kenneth Galbraith

It is not enough to be awake. One should also be alive!

When he dies he wants to be buried in Chicago or
Miami. He wants to participate in local politics
and vote.

Garbage in—garbage out.

Never buy a 'one of a kind' item at a 2-for-1 sale.
>—B.C. comics

THE GROSSER THE MOVIE THE GREATER THE GROSS.

This guy killed so many plants that there was wanted poster with his picture in every greenhouse in town.

Silence is a friend who will never betray.
>—Confucius

Riches are not forbidden, but the price of them is.
>—St. John Chrysostom

"He needed killin'" is a valid legal defense in some states.

Anyone who stops learning is old, whether at twenty or eighty. Anyone who keeps learning stays young.

—Henry Ford

The value of money is that with it you can tell anyone to go to the devil.

—Somerset Maugham

The liar's punishment is, not in the least that he is not believed, but that he cannot believe any one else.

——George Bernard Shaw

Honey lovers stick together.

A man murdered both parents and then pleaded for mercy on the grounds that he was an orphan.

—Abraham Lincoln

TO MAKE AMERICA WORK, AMERICANS WORKED.

We used to think about 15 minutes of fame. Now there's barely 15 minutes for lunch.

—P.C. Vey

Lawyer: A cat who settles disputes between mice.

You can say it with flowers, You can say it with candy, You can say it with jewelry or drink. You can say it with candles and dinner with brandy, But be sure you don't say it with ink.

May you live all the days of your life.

When the government puts teeth in the law, they aren't always wisdom teeth.

A man's respect for law and order exists in precise relationship to the size of his paycheck.

—Adam Clayton Powell, Jr.

If law school is so hard to get through, how come there are so many lawyers?

— Calvin Trillin

I think everybody is entitled to my opinion.

—Victor Borge

Some politicians get confused when they try to remember if they were born in a log cabin or a manger.

THE UPPER CRUST: A BUNCH OF CRUMBS HELD TOGETHER BY DOUGH.

One thing you will probably remember well is any time you forgive and forget.

—Franklin P. Jones

Money is not the key to happiness, but it unlocks interesting doors.

There must be quite a few things a hot bath won't cure, but I don't know of any of them.
—Sylvia Plath

Never panic when you get lost. Just change where it is you want to go.

When school is out, there's always the tearing up of homework, screeching and giggling. You would think professors would act more dignified.
—Paul Sweeney

If you want to be seen—stand up!
If you want to be heard—speak up!
If you want to be appreciated—shut up!

A political candidate must learn not only to stand on a platform, but to sit on the fence and lie on the spot.

—Frank Tyger

Success is relative. The more success, the more relatives.

There are still things you can get for a dollar — like nickels, dimes and quarters.

—Charles Lindner

HAPPINESS MAKES UP IN HEIGHT FOR WHAT IT LACKS IN LENGTH.

–ROBERT FROST

In show business, the key word is honesty. And once you've learned to fake that, you're in.

–George Burns

A diamond is just a lump of coal that stuck to its job.
—Leonardo da Vinci

Copper wire was invented when two lawyers were arguing over a penny.

Most new books are forgotten within a year,
especially by those who borrow them.
—Evan Esar

Better to go alone than to be accompanied by fools.

The world is so full of a number of things, I'm sure we
should all be as happy as kings.
—Robert Louis Stevenson

To live outside the law you must be scrupulously up to
code.
—Bob Dylan

You know you're in the Deep South when "ya'll" is singular and "all ya'll" is plural.

To learn to be a bullfighter, you must first learn how to be a bull.

Happiness is the meaning and the purpose of life, the whole aim and end of human existence.

—Aristotle

GOOD FENCES MAKES GOOD NEIGHBORS.

—ROBERT FROST

Happiness comes of the capacity to feel deeply, to enjoy simply, to think freely, to risk life, to be needed.

—Storm Jameson

Do not corner something that you know is meaner than you are.

Half the time things are better than normal—half the time things are worse than normal.

If you're a poker player you better develop a poker face.

May you live as long as you want and never want as long as you live.

—Irish blessing

The murals in restaurants are on a par with the food in museums.

—Peter DeVries

A portrait is a painting with something wrong with the mouth.

—John Singer Sargent

Failures don't plan to fail; they fail to plan.

—Harvey Mackay

Abstract art is a product of the untalented, sold by the unprincipled to the utterly bewildered.

—Al Capp

WE DON'T DRESS FOR WHO WE ARE, SO MUCH AS WHO WE WOULD LIKE TO BE.

—KATHLEEN TESSARO

Elegance is a sort of harmony that rather resembles beauty with the difference that the latter is more often a gift of nature and the former a result of art.

—Genevieve Antoine Dariaux

People aren't interested in you. They're interested in themselves.

—Dale Carnegie

Happiness is excitement that has found a settling down place, but there is always a little corner that keeps flapping around.

—E. L. Konigsburg

We may all have stopped smoking, but we continue to burn.

—Luc Sante

The list of the Ten Best Dressed Women is also the list of the Ten Hungriest Women.

—Genevieve Antoine Dariaux

The shrewd guess, the fertile hypothesize, the courageous leap to a tentative conclusion.

—Jerome Butler

Blue, red, yellow and green are lovely colors when they're kept apart, but mix them altogether and you just get brown.

Don't sell the bearskin before you kill the bear.

Life isn't about how fast you run, or how high you climb, but how well you bounce.

DYSLEXIA MEANS THAT YOU NEVER HAVE TO SAY YOU'RE YRROS.

If you think you're a person of some influence, try ordering somebody else's dog around.

FRIENDSHIP IS LIKE MONEY, EASIER MADE THAN KEPT.

—SAMUEL BUTLER

Locker room lore says that the name golf arose by default—all the other four-letter words had been taken.

—George Peper

Don't bother me. I'm living happily ever after.

Good sports knows their place, accept things at face value, lose gracefully, keep trying or take their toys and run home.
—Kathleen Tessaro

The art of taxation consists in so plucking the goose as to obtain the largest possible amount of feathers with the smallest possible amount of hissing.
—Jean-Baptiste Colbert

Good judgment comes from experience, and a great deal of that comes from bad judgment.

Timing has a lot to do with the outcome of a rain dance.

At 20, we worry about what others think of us; at 40, we don't care what they think , at 60 we discover they haven't been thinking of us at all.
—Bob Hope

FORGIVE YOUR ENEMIES. IT MESSES UP THEIR HEADS.

Courage is doing something frightening
when you have a choice of not doing it.
                    —Barbara Shulgasser-Parker

If it weren't for that last minute, nothing would ever get done.

Always end the name of your child with a vowel, so that when you yell, the name will carry.
                    —Bill Cosby

If it's good, they'll stop making it.

A successful marriage involved never asking too straight a question, and in never answering it fully, always leaving that tiny margin of unknowing.
                    —Elizabeth Buchan

You can get a lot more done with a kind word and a laugh than with a kind word alone.
                    —Al Capone

When in charge, ponder; when in trouble, delegate; when in doubt, mumble.

—James Boren

If it jams, force it. If it breaks, it needed replacing anyway.

—Wm. Lowery

Something happens to a man when he puts on a necktie. It cuts off all the oxygen to his brain.

—A.J. Carothers

MURPHY'S LAW: ANYTHING THAT CAN GO WRONG, WILL.

–EDWARD MURPHY, JR.

People will accept your idea much more readily if you tell them Benjamin Franklin said it first.

—David H. Comins

The shortest distance between two points is under construction.

—McGregor

Whatever creates the greatest inconvenience for the largest number of people tends to happen.

—Leonard Koppett

Those who rise to executive positions lack the qualifications for anything lower.

—Peter Ustinov

One out of 312 Americans is a bore, and a healthy male adult bore consumes each year one and half times his own weight in other people's patience.

—John Updike

It doesn't matter what you do, as long as you don't do it in public and frighten the horses.

—Mrs. Patrick Campbell

Life is like a roll of toilet paper. The closer it gets to the end, the faster it goes!

Egotism is the anesthetic that dulls the pain of stupidity.

—Frank Leahy

The worst drivers are either idiots and maniacs. Idiots include anyone who drives slower than we do, and maniacs are everyone who drives faster than we do.

TOO MANY FREAKS, NOT ENOUGH CIRCUSES.

Happiness comes of the capacity to feel deeply, to enjoy simply, to think freely, to risk life, to be needed.

—Storm Jameson

All time spent angry is time lost being happy.

—Mexican proverb

I can keep a secret. It's not that I'm morally superior. I just can't remember anything anyone tells me.

Follow the money. —Deep Throat

Money is ... the sixth sense which enables you to enjoy the other five.

—Somerset Maugham

A successful person is one who can lay a firm foundation with the bricks that others throw at him.

—David Brink

Opportunity is missed by most people because it is dressed in overalls and looks like work.

——Thomas Edison

Alcohol is the anesthesia by which we endure the operation of life.

—George Bernard Shaw

A cucumber should be well-sliced, dressed with pepper and vinegar, and then thrown out.

—Samuel Johnson

CHAOS, PANIC AND DISORDER— MY WORK HERE IS DONE.

Use a dictionary. Even if it you can't find a word because you can't spell it.

Eat what you like and let the food fight it out inside.

—Mark Twain

A musical talent is like having six fingers on one hand. You're born with it, you're different because of it, you can't do a thing about it.

—Florian Zabach

Don't do good that could look bad.

—Mexican proverb

To be ignorant of what occurred before you were born is to remain always a child.

—Cicero.

When two egotists meet, it's an I for an I.

Dancing is the perpendicular expression of a horizontal desire.

Money, horse racing and women; three things the boys just can't figure out.

—Will Rogers

Persons of ill will have feelings too, you know.

—Joanne Greenberg

Any day above ground is a good one.

An organization is a collection of choices looking for problems.

—Richard Mitchell

WHY IS THE WORD ABBREVIATION SO LONG?

Slovenly language makes it easier for
us to have foolish thoughts.
—George Orwell

If you can't face it, at least try to fake it.

Imagine what they'll be able to do when the training
wheels come off Congress.

Of all the things I've lost, it's my mind I miss the
most.

"Super-prompt critical power excursion." That's what the
AEC called a meltdown at Three Mile Island in 1978

There are many forms of stupidity and cleverness is the
worst.
—Thomas Mann

Book-writing makes horse racing seem like a solid, stable business.

—John Steinbeck

Experience is what you get when you don't get what you want.

Why do the airlines explain that what's supposed to be a direct flight but has a stopover is called a nonstop?

WHAT LIGHT? SOME OF US ARE STILL LOOKING FOR THE TUNNEL.

Just when you thought you were winning the rat race along comes a faster rat.

A perfect wife is one who doesn't expect a perfect husband.

Middle aged people shouldn't eat health foods. We

need all the preservatives we can get.

Dogs look up to you, cats look down on you.
—Winston Churchill

Anybody who gets away with something will come back
to get away with a little more.
—Harold Schonberg

I'll unscramble the eggs if you read me the recipe
backwards.

The rat race is OK, but we'd like a little
more cheese.

Imagination is more important than knowledge.
—Einstein

WHEN YOUR DREAMS TURN TO DUST—VACUUM.

Don't worry about the world ending
today—today is tomorrow in Australia.

Have a blast while you last.

There is nothing so stupid as an educated man if you
get him off the thing that he was educated in.
                                        —Will Rogers

Doing something stupid once is just plain dumb. Doing it
often is a philosophy.
                                        —Don Lancaster

Highbrow: a person who listens to the William Tell
overture and doesn't think of the Lone Ranger.

I have never heard of anyone stumbling on
something sitting down.
                                —Charles F. Kettering

Sometimes even mechanics cars break down.

Should businesses that don't have a profit list it as a negative deficit?

HE HAD DELUSIONS OF ADEQUACY.
                                    — WALTER KERR

```
Drinking drivers, nothing worse, they
put the quart before the hearse.
                        —Burma Shave
```

He is not only dull himself, he is the cause of dullness in others.
                                    — Samuel Johnson

We may be the only phone company in town, but we try not to act like it.
                                    —Bell Telephone System

Sense doesn't necessarily come before age.

A good friend's eye is a very good mirror. —Irish proverb

A law firm is successful when it has more clients than partners.

—Henny Youngman

They never open their mouths without subtracting from the sum of human knowledge.

—— Thomas Brackett Reed

A good soup attracts chairs.

In order to avoid being called a flirt, she always yielded easily.

—— Charles, Count Talleyrand

A SHEEP IN SHEEP'S CLOTHING.
— WINSTON CHURCHILL, ON CLEMENT ATLEE

How can you be an optimist if you're not willing to bet against the odds?

What you eat standing up doesn't count.   —Beth Barnes

The telephone is a good way to talk to people without having to offer them a drink.
                                        —Fran Lebowitz

He that drinks beer, thinks beer.

It is not necessary to advertise food to hungry people, fuel to cold people, or houses to the homeless.
                                        —J.K. Galbraith

A flying machine for people who can't stand heights.
                          —Pontiac auto advertisement

Soup is by its nature eccentric; no two are ever alike, unless of course you get soup from cans.
                                        —Laurie Colwin

Who writes the contract controls the negotiation.

—Rich Schell,

One pleasure of the cook is that now and then you learn all over again.

—Frances Mayes

LACK OF MONEY IS THE ROOT OF ALL EVIL.
—GEORGE BERNARD SHAW

I have everything I had twenty years ago, only it's all a little bit lower.
—Gypsy Rose Lee

Idleness is never enjoyable unless there is plenty to do.

Love makes the world go round? Not at all. Whisky makes it go round twice as fast.

—Compton Mackenzie

He who laughs last, thinks slowest.

Everything is funny as long as it is happening to somebody else.

—Will Rogers

For every action there is an equal and opposite reaction.

—Newton's Third Law

Happy the hare at morning, for she cannot read the hunter's waking thoughts.

—W.H. Auden

Better to wear out than to rust out.

—Bishop R. Cumberland

Procrastination is the art of keeping up with yesterday.

—Don Marquis

LOVE YOUR ENEMY—BUT DON'T PUT A GUN IN HIS
HAND.

His imagination resembled the wings
of an ostrich. It enabled him to run,
though not to soar.

— Lord Macaulay

Everyone lives by selling something.

—Robert Louis Stevenson

The true use of speech is not so much to express our
wants as to conceal them.

—Oliver Goldsmith

Don't drink and drive. You might spill your drink.

There is no money in poetry, but then there's no poetry in
money either.

—Robert Graves

Money. You don't know where it's been, but you put it where your mouth is. And it talks.

—Dana Gioia

The meek may inherit the earth—but not its mineral rights.

—J. Paul Getty

We are what we remember.

No more tears now; I will think about revenge.

—Mary, Queen of Scots

DON'T FORCE IT, GET A LARGER HAMMER.

Middle age is when your broad mind and narrow waist change places.

A penny saved is a penny to squander.

A person knows he's getting older when his back goes out more than he does.

Necessity knows no law.   —St. Augustine

Love is like infinity...that's the way I think love is, too.
                                                    —Mr. Rogers

Birds are entangled by their feet and men by their tongues.
                                                    —Thomas Fuller

It's better to know nothing than to know what ain't so.

                                        —Josh Billings

It ain't not bad.   —Bart Simpson

The effectiveness of any meeting is proportionally contrary to the size of the committee.

EIGHTY PERCENT OF SUCCESS IS SHOWING UP.
—WOODY ALLEN

We call an overdraft at the bank a non-performing asset.
—James Boren

A little inaccuracy sometimes saves tons of explanation.
—Saki

Inside every big problem is a small problem trying to get out.
—Don Lancaster

Anybody can win, unless there happens to be a second entry.
—George Ade

Elegance can *be* acquired only at the price of numerous errors that are *best* remembered with good humour.
—Genevieve Antoine Dariaux

Any tool, when dropped, will roll to the least accessible corner.

—Anthony

She was so brainless that her brain was a Grand Canyon of bewilderment, but you just had to admire her for its sheer size.

Don't worry, be happy.   —Bob Marley

Some people so shallow that when you look a second time you find out that they aren't really there.

```
If it's free, it's advice;
If you pay for it, it's counseling;
If you can use either one, it's a
miracle.
```

SMIRK

BIBLIOGRAPHY

Anonymous

Best Things Anybody Ever Said, Robert Byrne

Can't Believe you said That, William Cole

Carnival of Wit, Leo Rosten, *Plume Publishing*

Classified Communication, *Agnes Franz*

Comedians' Quote Book, Mallory & Rose, *Sterling Publishing*

The Crown Treasury of Relevant Quotations, Edward F. Murphy, *Crown Publishers*

Dimboxes, Epopts and Quotes, David Grambs, *Workman Press*

Eleganc,e Tessaro, Kathleen , *W,. Morrow*

Funny Accent, Barbara Shulgasser-Parker, *Picador USA*

Great Quotes from Great Women, Peggy Anderson, *Celebrating Excellence Publishing*

Guinness Book of Poisonous Quotes, Colin Jarman, *Contemporary Books*

Here at The New Yorker, Brendan Gill, *DaCapo Press*

Hitting the Sweet Spot, Lisa Fortini-Campbell, *Bending Communication*

IMP, Bob Westenberg

Is Sex Necessary? James Thurber and E. B. White

Leo's 100, Leo Burnett , *N T C Books*

NTC Dictionary of Quotes, Robin Hyman, *National Textbook Co.*

New Quotable Woman, Elaine Partnow, *Median Publishing*

Oxford Dictionary of Quotations, *Oxford University Press.*

Phrases Sayings and Quotes, *Oxford Press*

Poetry of Business Life, Ralph Windle *Berrett-Koehler*

The Power of Style, Taper and Edkins

Quotable Einstein, Alice Calaprice, *Prineton University Press*

Quotable Woman, *Running Press*

Selected Poetry of Ogden Nash, *Black Dog & Leventhal*

Unwritten Laws Hugh Rawson, *Crown Publishers*

Vegetable Heaven, Mollie Katzen

What Fresh Hell is This? Marion Meade, *Penguin Books*

Wild Words. Wild Women, Autumn Stephens, *Conari Press*

Order another copy of

S M I R K
Over 1450 Smiles for Your Face

from:

(888) 280-7715 or **Amazon.com**